May the Lord bless
you richly —

Jane Lamber

Isaiah 58:11

GLEANINGS

from a well-watered garden

Gleanings

from a well-watered garden

by

JANE W. LAUBER

Illustrations by the Author

THE GOLDEN QUILL PRESS
Publishers
Francestown   New Hampshire

Library of Congress Catalog Card Number 82-80286

ISBN 0-8233-0344-6

Printed in the United States of America

to

Stephen Burtis,
Pamela Jane
and
Stephen Robert

"I have no greater joy than to hear
that my children walk in truth."

(III John 4)

ACKNOWLEDGMENTS

Grateful acknowledgment is made to the following, in which some of the poems included in this book were first published:

Christian Herald: "Dress-Up," "Lord, Clean Me Quickly."

Christianity Today: "The Soldier," "Suffering," "Submission," "Wedding Dress."

Eternity: "The Thorn," "Simon Peter's Soliloquy," "Simon Says," "Discoveries" (with drawing of shepherd's hand), "Today," "Cleansing," "Free Captives." Reprinted by permission of *Eternity* Magazine, Copyright 1981, Evangelical Ministries, Inc., 1716 Spruce Street, Philadelphia, PA 19103.

Zondervan Publishing House: "Suffering" (in *Sourcebook of Poetry* compiled by Al Bryant).

CONTENTS

GLEANINGS

He has planted me by His River, sent His rains upon me in due season, and tenderly cultivated my life, so that anything that has grown, worthy of gleaning, is of His doing, and for His glory.

JUST WONDERING . . .

Did you ever wake and wonder
Why winds roar and thunders thunder?
Though "God of Peace," it still would seem —
Even *He* must let off steam!

GOOD NEWS?

The birds are singing — well, I bet
They haven't read the papers yet —
Or else they saw a supplement,
Or heard report from Heaven sent.

Perhaps — enough, to have today —
To feel the sun — to know the way
To build a nest — the way to fly —
With their example, Lord, may I
Rejoice — because You rule this day —
No matter what the papers say!

SPRING THAW

As winter earth contains the seed —
Yet   Spring — its life displays —
Holy Spirit — in my soul —
    dispel my cold
    and swell within my frame.

'Til winter earth within me yields
and parts as Power moves
to Light. So Christ shall bloom —
    Spring winds shall bear
    the fragrance of His name.

BEFORE THE COURT

Swollen buds
with dust of pearl
catch Spring sun
and further swell.
Their lustrous tones
of pinks and greens —
appropriate
to Queenly dress.

And upon
His scepter's touch,
rose velvet leaves
unfold
before the Court.

Yet we —
oblivious —
demeaningly declare
this oak as *"scrub"*
What nerve!
Excuse us, Lord.

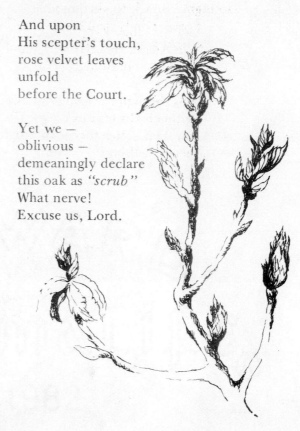

GALLERY TOUR

God walks His woods within my frame —
As once He strolled through Eden's lanes
He walks — in me.

Though this, a fallen Paradise
And I, a fallen Eve —
With Adam, He accompanied —
But now — indwells.

Thus through the gallery of His art
We touch His textures, view His forms —
And then — together — in delight
Declare it *"good!"*

15

UNWELCOME

Sorrow, Sorrow, Worm of life,
Routing trails as you intrude,
Burrowing between my roots!
Left a choice, I would exclude
Your ugly presence altogether, from my sphere —

Yet, you are here —

Bruising thus my being's depths
By some mysterious decree.
Accomplish that divine intent
For which you were assigned to me.
Loosen, aerate, and leave! Let heal; let grow —

Go quickly! Go!

SUFFERING

If flowers reasoned, would they understand
Why suddenly the gardener's hand
    Uproots
    Selects,
    Transplants
To give their roots more room, their leaves more air —
Would flowers misconstrue this care
    As wrath,
    Contempt,
    Disdain?
Or be content to let their beauty show
His wisdom . . . or demand to know
    His plan,
    Intent,
    Design?

THE MINT BED

Mint's intent — to *cover* earth —
Its lengthy longitude and girth —
Assigned but bit part in the play,
It nabs the leading role away!
Though just an herb for tea or such
As needs a spice or garnish touch . . .
As band barbarian invades
A hapless hamlet, mint parades
O'er daisies, phlox, petunias, kale —
Whatever else cannot prevail
Against the conquering minty horde.
I'll take my trusty trowel-sword
And *stop* expansionist assault!
At *my* set limit, mint must halt!

Dear Lord, may no activity
However fine a spice it be —
Take over. Spoil Thy Plan's intent —
And turn my life to mass of mint.

BOUNDARIES

Stone wall deliniations
Pronounce the same as He
Who spoke the world's arrangement
Dividing land and sea;
Defined and separated;
Partitioned night from day;
Set limits for the nations;
Prescribed behavior's way —
Compressed the mass of mountains
And smoothed the silky plain
Until the sculptured scenery
Distinctive form attained.

These rows of stone are altars raised,
As boundaries, agreeing
With Him Who laid the layered earth
And spoke it into being.

DEFACED

In God's studio I see
His masterpiece — the earth —
Rainbows, reaches glistening —
Bright beauty giving birth . . .
Until — defaced by marks of man —
With brother killing brother —
Dark smudges smeared by children's hand —

He'll have to paint another!

FREE CAPTIVES

"If the Son . . . shall make you free,
ye shall be free indeed."

(John 8:36)

Lethargic clumps of rusty algae
    line stone ledges on the coast of Maine,
And lie in listless strings while waiting
    for the tide, from which they will regain
Vitality and animation —
    Exposed to open skies, they are not free —
Until — submerged and inundated
    they become the captives of the sea.

21

TODAY

As drops assembled in a rushing wave
are soon dispersed, and never reconvene —
This group of rushing moments called "today"
breaks on the shore and never comes again.

RESISTANCE

Great boulders which comprise the ramparts of a shore
Seem stubbornly resistant to the sea,
  Yet meet continually unaltered action's will
  Until — the rocks are pebbles; pebbles, sand —
And sand is swept away beneath the tide.

When stone defenses on the shoreline of my soul
Determine to resist Thy seas of Grace,
  Persist in pulverizing unsubmissive will
  Until — my rocks are pebbles; pebbles, sand —
And all the sands of self are lost in Thee.

CLEANSING

"No chastening . . . seemeth joyous, but grievous,
nevertheless afterward it yieldeth the . . . fruit
of righteousness."

(Hebrews 12:11)

The waves are slammed against the shore relentlessly —
    and ripped apart —
But when retreating, leave
a progress line of weeds and sludge upon the shore —
    returning, cleansed.

EARLY AND LATTER RAINS

At Pentecost, the *early* rain
Prepared the Church for growth;
The *latter* rain will ripen grain
Before the scythe goes forth.

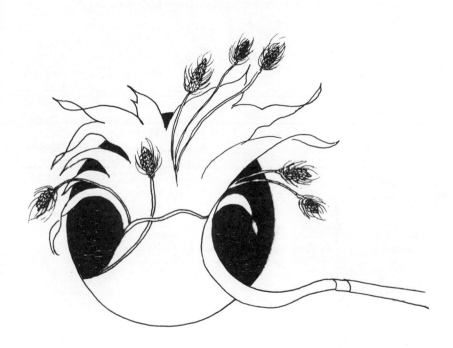

GRAND FINALE

Earth doesn't move to winter softly,
But with crescendo loud and lofty —
Its brilliant, fiery tones entirely
Lavish — for the Grand Finale.

I wonder if the Church, like autumn,
Her closing score's profuse display
Will dazzle earth with blazing glory
Before her leaves have blown away.

"Arise, shine; for thy light
is come, and the glory of the Lord
is risen upon thee. For, behold, the
darkness shall cover the earth, and
gross darkness the people; but the
Lord shall arise upon thee, and his
glory shall be seen upon thee."
(Isaiah 60:1-2)

SUNSET SYMBOL

Revival fires — like sunset
   may streak the sky with light
Before the vice-gripped earth succumbs
   to Tribulation night.

"MY YOKE IS EASY; MY BURDEN IS . . ."
(Matthew 11:30)

like snow dust
laid on branches —
pure,
enhancing,
light.

ENCOUNTER

How innocence must wince upon
a child's first sin!
As snow — unblemished, white succumbs
to earth's first stain —
      dog's yellow urine
      or man-stamped lane
      of resurrected mud
      (a vandal scribble over
      fine design blue shadows made)
      or furnace phlegm
      coughed black
      and spit on purity . . .
So earth imprints its mark on snow
and innocence.

WHY, NATURE —

You're wearing Sunday clothes to closet prayer!
For silver filigree cannot compare
To ice-encrusted limbs against the sky;
Yet here, remote within these woods, no eye
But only His — and sometimes mine — can see
Your dress. Then Nature whispers back to me,

    "What other ways
    than Beauty be
    appropriate
    to Praise?"

DRESS-UP

Lord, You must smile
  to see Your own,
  dressed up
  in piety . . .
Like little girls
  in mothers' clothes
  pretending what they're not —
  but hope to be.

UNABRIDGED

Theology defines —
Set categories stated —
Full definitions given
Of God and man related.

But I suspect that God,
Exceeding Revelation —
Has larger Dictionary
With broader explanation.

"THE UNKNOWN TONGUE"

Discreet of God, to find a way
  without disclosure, I may pray —
His perfect plan for you pursuing —
  knowing not what you've been doing!

TREASURE HUNT

"As earth's deep secrets we explore,
We find an awesome treasure store —
Like treasures hid within a chest,
Awaiting our scientific quest.
Here, we've discovered thus and so . . .
Vast treasures human minds now know
Because of our intelligence,
Our research skills and diligence."

"We're grateful! You've discovered much
Of long-sought facts on such and such . . .
But on *this* question have you hit —
This treasure chest — *who buried it?*"

PREFERENCE

I think I'd like the Maine coast, Lord —
  When Judgment has subsided —
When plowshares will be formed from swords,
  And Earth — to saints, divided.

WHAT JOSEPH MIGHT HAVE SAID
(but thankfully, didn't)

"Visions? dreams? interpretations?
What are these so-called 'revelations?'
Perhaps in early days were needed
But surely now are superceded!"

"You mention seven cows of fat?
Now Pharaoh, tell me where you're at —
The lean ones ate the fat ones up?
I wonder what was in your cup!"

"Though I am sure hard times are coming —
No need to panic, or be dumb in
Sounding like a doom and gloomer . . .
We'll call the famine just a rumor!"

"We'll take our ease. We'll not prepare . . .
For even if it comes we'll dare
Our humane God to undertake
And He will feed us filet steak!"

NOT SO STRANGE

Squirrels have always "squirreled away"
And ants prepare against the day
Of winter cold. In days of old
When the judgment was foretold,
Even sane and sober Noah
Made provision for the Pour!
And, freezers, jars, and dehydrators
Serve as winter insulators.

If you feel that winter's near —
(The Judgment Winter sent to clear
The ravaged earth for Rampant Spring
Which Millennium will bring) —
It's really not too odd, it seems,
To put up produce, lay up beans!

WHO, LORD?

The love of many shall wax cold
    and many "fall away"
With faith denied and names erased
    before the Final Day.

Naught can grow cold, but once was warm,
    "depart" but which was placed —
And names in jeopardy must be
    inscribed, to be erased.

I wonder who, within this pew
    will fall — will abdicate,
Denying Him whose love they knew —
    Allegience terminate.

As long ago, in Upper Room,
    one hears a piercing cry,
(When told that one would fall away)
    "Lord, who? Lord, is it I?"

(Matthew 24:12;
II Thessalonians 2:3;
Revelation 3:5)

PAINTER'S ANNOYANCE

This brush won't *bend*
as brushes should!
for paint is hard between the hairs —
it's useless to me now —
except to stir . . .

Could I be such a brush, my Lord?
with wrongs solidified?
Put me to soak!
Then rinse me clean —
That in Your atelier and Hand
I may be used —
a supple brush
performing
holy artistry.

CLEAN ME, LORD

Lord, clean me quickly —
    Wash out my spots
    My frequent stains
    Before they set.

    Sweep up the soil
    That muddy thoughts
    Track through my mind.

    Deliver me
    From ground-in dirt!

THE JOY OF THE LORD

I searched His many rooms for joy —
His corridors at length,
For often I had read, "His joy
    shall be your strength."

Yet weariness ran with me;
Frustration was my friend —
Though in His house — His joy remained
    concealed. But then . . .

"Stop running through my house!" He called.
"Stand still, my Child — Believe.
My joy is not for you to *find* —
    but to *receive*."

"Then *You* I seek, my Lord!" I cried —
And turning, wept to see
His Spirit, serving *trays* of joy —
    at last — located me!

NOAH'S ARK

The door was shut by God —
Safety's guarantee —
The only window faced,
Not toward the surging sea,
But Heavenward its view —
Direction — fear allays —
Oriented to the Throne,
Not circumstance, nor waves.

OUTLINE

The light which rims my window shade
Confirms the dawn concealed —
Thy Word — the Light that lines our veil
'Til Morning be revealed!

BETHEL

Reason placed upon the Stone —
(As Jacob's head reclined,)
A sacrifice of Intellect —
Will "open heavens" find.

SIMEON'S RELEASE

"I've seen Him! Lord, I'm satisfied —
I've witnessed Thy Salvation —
With my own eyes I now behold
The Gentiles' Revelation!
I am released to leave this world,
In peace this life depart —
The Light that lightens nations
Now shines upon my heart."

So satisfied as Simeon,
I pray, Lord, may I be
Released from every worldly hold
With but one glimpse of Thee.

MIRACLE AT CANA

"... we have this treasure in earthen vessels ..."

(II Cor. 4:7)

To His command and filling
The vessels are released,
And water changes into wine
At Cana's marriage feast.

So, As He fills our vessels
With Water — as the Sign
Of Holy Spirit — when poured out
That Water turns to Wine!

SIMON SAYS . . .

"You want my boat?
Yes, Master, come, I'll shove it from the shore
so you may teach."
Then, to himself, complains,
"He interrupts
my necessary chores! They *must* be done!
But . . . I'll comply.
I feel I owe him this
for what he did —
with my wife's mother healed, this favor's small.
Just don't talk long!
Your world is one of words —
but mine is *work* —
a smelly scene where rotting entrails reek
from fish I clean,
where nets demand my time."

"You speak of Heaven.
And so may I someday, but not just yet!
For now my mind
pursues elusive fish
throughout this sea —
a nightly contest won by *them* last night . . .
but you don't know
discouragement like that,
nor how it feels
when shoulders ache from straining oars against
a vicious wind.
I'm tired! But you don't understand."

"At last, he's through!"
"What's that? You say go out *again* for fish!"
"I'll hold my tongue —"
"Yes, Master, we will go."

"He knows we've been
at this all night! I told him that! Then *why*
this futile trip?
I'll bow to his audacity
to show respect . . .
But can't he *see* — my rugged hands attest
my competence!
I know the ways of fish —
to search for them
by day — ridiculous! Yes, even such
a man of God
should stay within his field! "

"What pounds my boat?
What churns these waters, slaps the hull as some
sea monster's tail?
It's *fish*! We're riding *waves*
of countless *fish*!
Master! *FISH*! "

DIVINE DELAY

He waits 'til festive drink has ceased —
Until *good* wine is gone,
Before *His* vintage is released;
The *better* wine is drawn.

He waits until disciples ache,
Discouraged by the strain
Of fishing futilely, before
He speaks net-breaking gain.

"Delayed en route," despite the shout
For haste in Jarius' heart —
Dread Death performs; prepares the stage
For Jesus' master part.

He waited; Lazarus decomposed;
Wet grief assailed the wait.
But *wine*, and *catch* and *life* attest
He did not come too late.

ANOINTING PERFUME

Like Mary's nard, the Spirit's oil
In perfume, forms the part
Of blending base — with sorrow —
Crushed petals of my heart.

This costly essence of my soul,
I pour, Lord, on Your head —
But not as Mary, "unto death,"
But unto joy instead.

SUBMISSION

Although corralled in Grace,
My will still sometimes balks
And stomps and stamps the earth
And rears and flails and neighs
Defiance, for
The bit is hard.

Once, Lord, you rode
An untried colt —
Unbroken, yet for you,
Submissive — and it heard
Hosannas to your name!

O Lord, subdue —
I long to hear hosannas too!

"MY WILL" vs. "THY WILL"
(Luke 22:42)

Wrenching,
Desperate
Groans of conflict

                             Ricochet

   past flower heads —

                           off rocky walls —

which line the tortured battle field.
Gethsemane — the Garden War.

THE SOLDIER

The soldier's job is grim —

But strength is not revealed in easy tasks.
His hammer is to drive the heavy nails
Into the hands and feet of men who soon
Will curse him savagely, as death prevails.

A scene familiar now.

His duty soon begins.

Now hard, from knowing death's companionship,
Ignoring hatred in the eyes of two —
The soldier startles at the voice he hears,
"Forgive them, for they know not what they do."

Forgiveness from condemned?

He stands transfixed and stunned.

No sword could penetrate as do the eyes
At which the soldier stares; his heart is bound
Far tighter than his victim's yielding hands.
The spike is placed; the hammer's blows resound.

The task is soon complete.

The crosses then are raised.

As enemies revile and while friends weep,
He watches silently as Jesus dies.
One speaks, "This truly was the Son of God!"
The soldier's stoic countenance belies

The echo in his heart.

THE THORN

The thorn first grew in curse of
        stony ground surrounding
        Eden's once abundant lands

Where Adam basked in unbarbed
        beauty. Now sin's flower rips
        his bruised and weary hands.

An unknown hand removes a twisted
        crown from Jesus' brow, in
        which its spikes had pressed.

Again — the curse of stony, blood-
        stained ground, thorns lie discarded
        on Golgotha's crest.

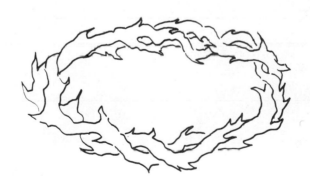

SIMON PETER, AFTER . . .

What is left?
Your Death's constricting sinews crush my soul
Ripped raw as slashed by claws
Of savage shame —
My dastardly denial — O my Lord!
My heart lies dead; my love for You remains
For love is not so fragile
As a heart.

DISCOVERIES

Once, humble shepherds peered with silent awe
    into a stable cave — discovering
The wonder of His presence, as they saw
    Immanuel.

Years later, two disciples raced, and gazed
    into an empty cave — discovering
The wonder of His absence, and they praised
    their living Lord.

AWAKE!

Five virgins lost, through short supplying,
The opening of the heavenly door —
One servant lost, through fear and hiding,
Rewards of ruling with the Lord.

Awake then, Zion, from your sleeping!
The Day approaches very near —
Go forth with lamps fresh-trimmed and shining —
The coming Bridegroom's calling, hear!

Though "Where is He?" the scoffers question;
"Where is He? He comes at last?
Where the promise of His coming?"
Even faithful ones shall ask.
"Where is He?"
Within my Being!
"Where His residence?"
My frame!
"Where His voice?"
My proclamation!
"Where His power?"
In His Name!

So speak, my Being, life and verbage —
Fearlessly of Jesus tell —
Speak His power to deliver
Souls from bondages and Hell!

Awake, anointed one, and stand,
Stand by Zerubbabel, the Lord —
With Spirit's power, great and mighty,
Move the mountains with The Word!

Who despised the "small beginnings"
Day of which has come and gone?
The Greater Day — its light has broken —
The Deluge of the world is on!

"Not by might" — Denominations —
Not by powers to persuade —
But by the Spirit's Demonstration
Through those anointed, unafraid,

Who hold the burning lamps of Witness,
By which light the path is shown
Through the doorway to the Marriage —
The Feast no human mind has known.

Arouse! Awake! Put on your armor!
Cast off your ease, complacency —
Awake, O Zion, to His coming —
The Thief — no sleeping eye shall see.

THE STONES CRY OUT

This silent churchyard would not be so hushed
Were tombstones given tongues —

For they would sing their temporary state
And choirs of marble monuments would chant,
"We wait the trumpet sound! For then this ground
Will tremble with a power earth once knew —
(A hidden memory within our veins)
Another stone — our prototype was moved;
Death's weight dislodged; the Resurrection proved."

"One day our polished faces will reflect
A holy light, as heavenly shapes ascend.
Amid the swirling mists, our empty biers
And toppled forms will mark a place of *life!*
(A hidden hope implanted in our veins)
For Christ will clear Death's atmosphere, destroy
Its gloom with winds of Resurrection joy!"

This silent churchyard would resound with songs,
Were tombstones given tongues.

WEDDING DRESS

"... to him that worketh not, but believeth ..."

(Romans 4:5)

You have your *work* clothes on, my Dear,
That simply will not do!
The Wedding's near! Please will you wear
The garments *bought* for you!

CLOUDS OF PROMISE

"Caught up . . . with them in the clouds . . . to
meet the Lord . . ."

(I Thessalonians 4:17)

Heavy clouds, hung low with waters —
Dark riders on the morning lane —
You hold more promise than of moisture —
You hold more hope than that of rain.
You hold expectancy of parting —
Parting for a holy train . . .
That bright procession placing palms
Of glory down — for Him to tread —
That shining chorus chanting psalms
Of victory unto their Head.

Heavy clouds, hung low with waters,
Part quickly, and reveal that view!
Perhaps today you'll fall to me —
Perhaps — I'll rise to you!